THE 9 LEVELS TO GREATER PROFITABILITY

HOW I TRIPLED NET PROFIT IN 12 MONTHS

PETER MUELLER

 FriesenPress

One Printers Way
Altona, MB R0G 0B0
Canada

www.friesenpress.com

ISBN
978-1-03-919351-2 (Hardcover)
978-1-03-919350-5 (Paperback)
978-1-03-919352-9 (eBook)

1. BUSINESS & ECONOMICS, STRATEGIC PLANNING

Distributed to the trade by The Ingram Book Company

DEDICATION

This book is dedicated to all the people who have inspired me in my real estate career, starting with my parents, Walter and Anne Mueller, as well as to all the trainers, coaches, and consultants that I have had the privilege to work with, who have enlightened me throughout the years.

I especially want to dedicate this book to Tacita Haynes and Angela Hoffmann. These two wonderful team members have been with me since the beginning of 2008 and have always believed in me and our vision. They never gave up on our dream of creating something special which we today call The Profit Centre.

TABLE OF CONTENTS

FOREWORD

I have always had a love for business consulting and have been blessed to share in many experiences all over the world. When Peter asked me to write a foreword for this book, I was honoured. Over our forty-five-year friendship, we both became experts in our own fields; his real estate coaching, and my business consulting for the top 100 firms in the world.

Over the years, Peter and I have had several conversations regarding the lack of business fundamentals and a balanced perspective in the real estate sector. As an agent and broker, Peter would brag about his sales volumes in a month or given year. I would then ask him, "How much money or profit did you make?" His answers were always less boisterous or specific. In other words, he wasn't sure or didn't even know. He and many of his colleagues were always focused on the sales aspect and thought, I am selling more, so I must be more profitable . . . right?

It wasn't until I showed him some profit and loss principles, that he realized that volume growth does not always equate to an increase in profit. We phrased this as The 2 Sides of the Coin. One side focused on sales and volumes, while the other focused on business operations/optimization, financials, and finally profit. It took him a while to really grasp what he had in front of him in black and white. However, when he did, the proverbial light went on in his head, and thus he began his MBA training in the School of Hard Knocks. He realized how much money, time, and effectiveness he had lost chasing sales volumes instead of profitability. We built a model and strategies for his own success, and then quickly realized we had something unique to his industry.

After years of tweaks and applying what he learned, Peter became a thought leader for his industry. His determination and motivation to bring focus on profitability is how Peter started on his journey of coaching, training, and consulting. To this day, he touches base with me to evolve his own methodologies and practices to continue helping others.

In conclusion, Peter's own journey is a relevant example of how someone with guidance and coaching has become more fulfilled and profitable via God's grace and a huge paradigm shift. Please take the time to

Peter Mueller

read Peter's journey and take that which is applicable to your situation.

Sincerely,
Werner Rodriguez
BTech, EMBA, MPM, SA, RTE, PhD (Honourary)

Mr. Rodriguez is a sought-after industry leader, providing senior-level expertise on strategic management solutions. With over thirty-five years of global Big 5 Consultancy and Financial Services leadership delivering strategic Business and Technology transformations.

INTRODUCTION

The 9 Levels to Greater Profitability was born out of my life experiences in the real estate industry. It's about the ups and the downs, the education, application, and evolution of the mindset that I developed learning from some of the brightest minds in the industry.

It is about the blessing of being in an industry that constantly promotes self-improvement through education, training, coaching, and consulting. I have been in that environment since I was nineteen years old.

This book is about my journey of learning and growth through the School of Hard Knocks. These hard lessons of life shaped me into becoming a more well-rounded businessperson even though I am hardwired to think like a salesperson. How great it was to realize that even though we are who we are, we can refine and adapt our behaviours—if we're open to it.

Profitability is probably the most elusive and misunderstood concept in any sales industry. I learned the hard way that making money and making profit are two different things. That inspired me to write a keynote presentation called:

> *"Stop Just Making Money and Start*
> *Building a Profitable Business."*

Like me, many agents in my office lived from commission cheque to commission cheque. What was especially interesting is that the agents in my office who were the most productive were the ones always getting cash advances leveraged on their transactions that were yet to close.

It is interesting when you look back at your life and see what brought you to where you are today. We all have our story, and we all have our journey. This story is about how I became a better coaching, and training business called The Profit Centre. It is almost absurd because, back in the day, I was the poster boy for how a salesperson acts. What I mean by that, if I would use an analogy of a car, a salesperson is the one who is the gas pedal, and the businessperson is the brakes. Not one is more important than the other.

A true salesperson is a doer, they get things done, they recruit, they sell, and they make things happen. A businessperson says wait for a second, let's fill up the gas tank before we leave and check the tires. The businessperson is the analyzer and the one who pumps the brakes when you are going headlong into a wall. I was never a businessperson in this context. My solution and philosophy back then was, as an agent, if I needed more money, I would just sell more houses. When I became a broker, my philosophy was to just recruit more agents.

When I am speaking on stage today, I know that at least seventy percent of my audience can relate to me one hundred percent.

The reality is that if we are going to run a business, we need to be a businessperson first. You need gas in the car, and air in the tires and yes, perhaps we can call that a plan, a strategy, or an approach.

I believe this is the reason why profitability is so elusive. We are in an industry predominantly made of sales-people. For some of us, our ambition drives us to con-sider starting a brokerage. When that is the case, we can find out quickly that running a business is not the same thing as sales. Sales is a function of running a business. Therefore, we need to evolve and learn how to be better businesspeople or be in partnership with someone who has natural businessperson skills and acumen.

This book's main theme and message is simply this: Just because you are a salesperson does not mean you can't also be a businessperson and try to implement the disciplines necessary for lasting success and profitability.

Through my years of experience, mistakes, and lessons while running my brokerage, I discovered a method that needs to be followed to achieve extraordi-nary results. More on that in a moment.

I wish I knew even half as much as I know now, especially when I sold my brokerage. I was young and naïve and had been unfairly taken advantage of. I know the devastating pain of being cheated out of hundreds of thousands of dollars.

My goal and mission is to prevent brokers from throwing in the towel or getting shortchanged from getting what they deserve for all the hard work and effort they have done. I want to show people that the solutions may not be so elusive and to see the possibilities.

In my day-to-day experience, I get to work and speak with some of the best in the industry and have learned so much from them as well. It is interesting to note how few people take advantage of the expertise that is available to them.

"Those that need me the most, hire me the least, and those that need me the least, hire me the most."
—Peter Mueller

The most successful people in this world understand that growth and success can come from learning from others in order to avoid the pitfalls and challenges that they have made.

My observations and experience helped me develop what I like to call my Profitability Business Model™.

The Profitability Business Model™ is comprised of 9 levels. I will share with you these 9 levels that I implemented in my brokerage whereby I tripled my net profit in twelve months—even after losing ten agents—and by not raising my fees.

Many may find this hard to believe because the solutions I found were not the obvious ones which were to raise fees and recruit more agents.

The starting point of the evolution of this approach came when my business coach at the time shared

with me a simple understanding. He told me the most important number of your brokerage is:

Gross Profit Per Agent (GPPA)

I will delve further into this concept later on in this book.

Please bear in mind, I am merely trying to share the fundamental aspects of the model and how it personally applied to me in my circumstances. I know that the fundamental framework will apply to your operations as well. Whether you are in North America, Europe, South America, or elsewhere, the same business fundamentals apply. It is universal.

My intention in writing this book is to make these business fundamentals easy to understand from a layperson's perspective. As you follow along with my story, you will then easily see how you can apply these same fundamentals to your business.

MY STORY

Sales have always been in my blood. As a child, I always found myself involved in making money in one form or another, whether it was the paper routes, lemonade stand, collecting beer bottles, or selling firecrackers at my school. By the way, I got into big trouble with my principal on that last one.

When you are young, you don't know who you are. There was no question that being good in sales would be something I would excel at. However, it wasn't something I consciously knew at that time to be a fundamental characteristic that would define me. I had no idea about personality types or characteristics.

I struggled in high school because I didn't understand those things. I had no clarity or vision. I had a combination of ADD and a lack of clear direction. I never had a teacher that had a significant influence on my life. I was floundering.

Looking back, it was obvious what the problem was. I lacked an understanding of who I was. I was taking courses like physics and chemistry in high school, and I only took those courses because those were the courses my friends enrolled in.

Back in the 80's, my parents were in real estate. I got my license and worked for them. I loved the real estate agent's lifestyle and was very accustomed to the crazy hours and the unstructured pace. My parents were very successful and living the lifestyle that was very appealing to me. My father thrived in that environment where he used his natural ability to charm and communicate. That consequently made him very successful.

It was cool discovering my true self when I was able to identify and discover that I shared some of the same qualities as my dad.

I got my real estate license when I was eighteen years old. I just started shaving at that time, and I looked sixteen. In my case, however, ignorance was truly bliss. It's a good thing that I never considered that anyone should take me seriously. I was oblivious. Good thing.

I bought my first house when I was nineteen, and I was so excited about the process. I still remember the day I was driving my mom to church, and we passed by a huge billboard advertising new homes for sale starting at $69,900. I freaked my mom out when I told her I was going to buy a new home. I learned enough about real estate to understand what it took to get financing and how much I would need to close the sale. I quickly determined that buying a house would cost me as much as rent did at the time, and I couldn't understand why anyone would want to rent. I didn't even have the down payment together. I only had the belief that I would have it in time for the closing date which was approximately nine months later.

I have always been excited and passionate about helping people get into a home, and that is what helped me become a good salesperson. In the '80s when waterbeds were popular, I was in a store and ready to buy one. In talking with the salesperson, I asked her if she owned a home. By the way, I didn't learn some smooth sales techniques here. I asked out of legitimate curiosity. When she told me she didn't but would love to, my response was, "I would love to help you." I sold her and her husband a house in the following weeks.

I ended up working for my parents' company, Anne Mueller Real Estate for approximately two years. I thrived with them, and I learned so much. It was fun hanging out with my dad and watching him spin his magic. I witnessed how diligent my mom was in dealing with the agents. As the broker, her mission was to have the cooperating agent's commission cheque written on the day of closing. She had a great reputation in the industry. You wanted to sell a Mueller listing. My parents were constantly an example to me of always giving more than what people would expect.

There came the time however, when I felt I needed to expand my horizons. I needed to find my own identity. I was always referred to as Walter or Anne's son. So, I decided to join a large real estate firm.

My mom was sad when I told her of my intentions, but she knew I would thrive in that kind of environment. Being around a lot of people gives me energy and I was so competitive. I was more motivated to be number one on the top ten list than I was for the money that it generated. Looking back, I realize that money wasn't a motivator for me, acknowledgement was. We are all different. Some may find that to be superficial, but we are who we are. It's important to be aware of what motivates you to be successful.

One day when I was at the office, an older gentleman who was always the top producer in the office approached me. I was the young upstart and, I suppose, the disrupter in the office. I was also the new top producer. They couldn't figure out how I was selling so many houses. He approached me one day and said to me, "I don't know if you know this Peter, but we are in a recession." I said to him, "A recession? What's a recession?" I honestly didn't know.

Cool lesson, however—never be influenced by market conditions and negativity. Remember the waterbed story? That lady that bought a house from me was originally not in the mindset to buy a house. I just gave her the help, direction, and belief that it was possible. So, stay positive and plow through any market! People have to buy and sell houses all the time, regardless of the market conditions. Somebody has to be their agent, why not you?

"When you fly high people will throw stones at you. Don't look down. Just fly higher so the stones won't reach you."
—Chetan Bhagat

Let's now talk about unpleasant things, the things that ultimately led me to write this book. Let's talk about the elephant in the room that affects at least seventy percent of the real estate agents in the industry, knuckleheads like me. I lacked financial management skills. Even though I "made" a lot of money, I didn't handle my money very well. I was an impulsive and emotional spender, and so I lacked the discipline to put money aside for the future or to follow a budget. Being profitable was not a state of mind for me.

I'll share a story that I believe will put the above into context. In the '80s when I started working in real estate in Toronto, Ontario, Canada, salespeople were treated as employees by their brokers. When we received a commission cheque, the broker would deduct the income tax and issue us a cheque for the amount after this deduction. There was one year when I received an $8,600 tax payment refund from the government. I thought I had died and gone to heaven. But the fact of the matter was, I had already paid the government close to $50,000.

When the government instituted the independent contractor status for real estate agents, we were elated. Why should the government force employers to collect our money? We were now made responsible to submit our own taxes. On paper, this looked like a great advantage to agents. In real life, it was a disaster.

The year we became independent contractors, I had a banner year in sales. I earned approximately

$250,000 in commissions which was an additional

$50,000 over the previous year. Now comes the gut punch. I owed taxes at the end of the year for more than $50,000. Let me put this into context if you are bad at math. That means I spent $100,000 more that year than the previous year. Are you kidding me? How is that possible? I think some of you that are reading this are starting to feel a little ill.

My story is not much different from others working in this industry, or shall we say any sales industry. Here is what my experience has taught me: The problem with the industry is that it is always focused on driving volume. More sales, convert more leads, get more listings, recruit more agents. Volume! Volume! Volume! The need was to focus on return on volume. If I had focused on that, I would have had a financial plan or budget in place. Putting money aside for my taxes would have been a no-brainer.

Management theorist Peter Drucker is quoted often as saying:

"What you measure gets improved."

That is certainly a true statement. Notice what always gets improved or focused on in the real estate industry—volume!

What's worse, is that when we strive for more, we work harder and spend less time at home with our family. To top it all off, we sometimes end up owing more.

What doesn't get measured is what's left over—profit. That is why so many struggle with profitability. It isn't taught, promoted, or even mentioned in the sales industry.

I enrolled in all the sales training available during my time and attended many conferences and events. I learned many skills and approaches, and I had many coaches. What I didn't realize was that I was not learning about how to keep my hard-earned money. I was only learning how to make more.

In 1994, when I was twenty-nine years old, I got the bright idea that I wanted to be a broker. That was an interesting journey. I put everything I had into this. It was a great and difficult learning experience. I built the office from the ground up and took on a lot of debt. I recall that I had spent $210,000 before I broke even.

I was a recruiting machine. I was on the phone for at least two hours a day, five days a week. My efforts paid off, and I recruited forty agents in my first twelve months. I then grew to sixty agents the following year. Once again, my primary focus was on recruiting (volume). I was not focused on profit.

I was extremely fortunate, however, in my career because I was blessed to have a couple of great business coaches in my life. They significantly helped me succeed because they were instrumental in changing my mindset.

I had a salesperson mindset. What I did not realize was that I needed to adopt a businessperson's mindset and in so doing that changed my life. I'll speak much more on that when I walk you through The 9 Levels to Greater Profitability and How I Tripled Net Profits in 12 months.

I successfully sold my business in 2003 after making it a very highly profitable venture. I thought I had done very well. Unfortunately, I sold my business to a scoundrel, and I never received compensation for all my hard work. He cheated me out of my payout. He was certainly a brilliant crook. He purchased my company through a holding company. When it came down to pay, he simply threatened to close the holding company which had no assets. I won't get into more details than that. That's too big a story. So now, my passion is born out of helping others not to make the same mistakes I made.

I have said many times, to many people, that I have a million-dollar education. I have learned more about what not to do, than what to do. I also learned that you should only do business with people that are honest and have integrity.

"Success is walking from failure to failure with no loss of enthusiasm."
—*Winston Churchill*

Putting that aside, I decided to dedicate myself to helping brokers, teams, and agents understand profitability and how that relates to their business. It is also a passion of mine to help brokers prepare their businesses to sell.

That is what inspired me to found The Profit Centre in 2008.

THE PROFIT CENTRE

The inception of The Profit Centre was certainly born out of my personal experiences—successes and failures. My main focus is to help my clients become better businesspeople and focus on profit.

I was annoyed that everyone was teaching the same things. I was frustrated because I saw that the only thing being promoted was training on volume. Why was the return on volume so elusive and so rarely discussed?

OUR MISSION STATEMENT:

To passionately enhance people's lives by guiding them towards greater profitability.

At The Profit Centre, we believe that it makes no sense to keep promoting more sales and recruiting more agents unless you also get a handle on building your business like a business. It's about thinking more like a businessperson and not just like a salesperson.

As business consultants in the real estate industry, we have worked with over one thousand offices throughout the world, and we have accumulated extensive knowledge about and insights into the brokerage business.

Based on this consulting experience we have accumulated and organized our services into what we believe to be the most exhaustive and powerful brokerage profitability coaching, consulting, and training in the industry.

We have helped brokerages, teams, and agents significantly improve their bottom line. We've also helped many of them sell their businesses for millions of dollars.

OUR VISION:

To become a global organization that changes the mindset of those in the real estate industry by focusing on profitability rather than just making money.

I have accumulated hundreds of testimonials worldwide on how this theme resonated with their lives and we will not deviate from this message. It is my ardent belief that if we focus on profit first, we will make more money and live better lives.

I would be lying if I didn't tell you that this message has felt like swimming upstream for several years. Large franchise corporations that want to serve their brokers and agents are usually persuaded to provide speakers and training focused on driving more volume.

My concrete belief is that if you focus on building a business and have a plan in becoming more profitable you will not only drive more volume, but you will also live a better life.

When you focus on the profit you are consequently also building equity. This is something that does not get enough attention. The greater the profitability, the more valuable the business, because you are creating equity.

Equity is what you sell it for.

THE 5 PURPOSES
OF A BUSINESS

The 5 Purposes of a Business are the guiding principles to pursue when building a thriving business.

When I took some time to consider and define the purposes, I thought in terms of the sequential order of those purposes.

PURPOSE 1: TO MAKE A PROFIT

The first purpose of a business is to make a profit. I know that that may sound kind of obvious, however, the reality is that many brokers struggle with profitability. There is a big difference between making money and making a profit. I know many brokers that make a lot of money, but they are not as profitable as they could be.

Another issue is how you define profit. From The Profit Centre's position, profit is what is left over after you:

- pay yourself your own sales commissions as an agent of your office
- pay yourself a normalized salary (with benefits) if you are an employee of your office
- pay yourself the equivalent of market rent if you own the building your office is in

To define profit appropriately you need to analyze and look at your numbers from what I like to call, the view of a buyer.

I like using this term because it helps one visualize the standard we need to agree on.

At the time of publishing this book, The Profit Centre has analyzed more than one thousand offices worldwide. For our analysis to have validity, we had to create a standardized method to create an apples-to-apples comparison.

PURPOSE 2: LEVERAGE

The second purpose of a business is leverage. Leverage gives you freedom, opportunity, and time to focus on your vision and potentially build an empire.

What that means is that your business needs to be built to run with or without you running the day-to-day operations. It's about your business being systems dependent and not people dependent (or dependent upon you).

Your business should be guided by a set of systems, processes, and procedures that anyone can follow.

Therefore, profit is the first purpose of a business. Without profit how can you possibly hire the team you need to be successfully leveraged?

PURPOSE 3: DIFFERENTIATE

Every business needs to have clearly defined points of differentiation. Without differentiation, we will always be subject to price. A good example of differentiation is cars. All cars can get you from A to B, however, some cars may get you there in style or get you there quicker. You would never dream of walking into a BMW dealership and buying one of their cars for the same price as a Volkswagen. It never fails to amaze me how some are willing to pay a higher price for the sake of exclusivity and quality.

You need to define who you are and the market you want to serve. Some brokers try to be all things to all people. That will always be a losing proposition because you will ultimately jeopardize and water down your integrity.

PURPOSE 4: PROFESSIONAL FULFILLMENT

Enjoyment of your life is important. Life is not fun if everything you do is a grind. Waking up in the morning and looking forward to going to work is a great feeling. That feeling is energizing and will help you do what you need to do to succeed.

What does professional fulfillment look like to you? It can mean different things for different people. It's on you to know what brings you that joy.

Establishing a vision and seeing it come to life is very fulfilling. True fulfillment comes when the business you are creating is thriving and built on a solid foundation.

Focusing on the creation of equity is especially fulfilling when you have a plan and an approach that you know will contribute to your mission and vision.

PURPOSE 5: TO HAVE SOMETHING TO EVENTUALLY SELL

Whether you want to die in the business or ultimately sell it, the purpose of a business is to build it as if you want to sell it. If we don't look at the business from that perspective, the question should be asked, why are we doing it?

As I mentioned earlier, when we focus on profitability, we are ultimately creating equity. Equity is the foundation of creating wealth. It is the ultimate leverage.

I have had the privilege of contributing to building profitability and facilitating the sale of numerous businesses since The Profit Centre's founding. It is a thrill to help our clients sell their businesses for $1,000,000+ dollars.

THE 2 SIDES OF THE COIN IN MANAGING PROFIT

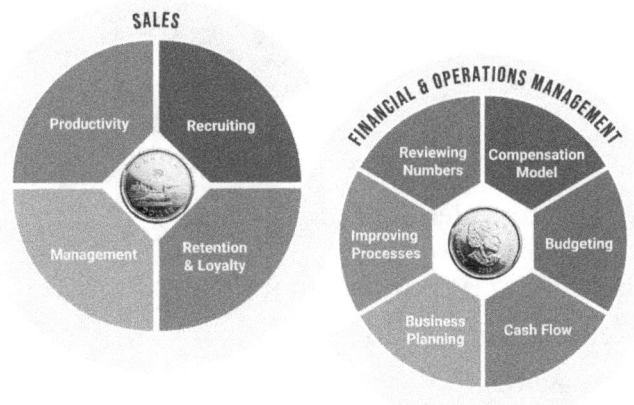

I learned the concept of The 2 Sides of the Coin to managing profit from my friend and mentor, Werner Rodriguez, who wrote the foreword to this book.

The 2 Sides of the Coin are the SALES side and the FINANCIAL & OPERATIONS MANAGEMENT side. Both sides of the coin need to be addressed to create a profitable business.

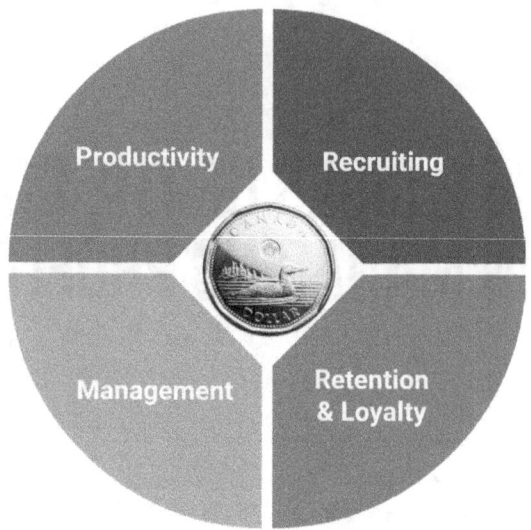

The SALES side of the coin involves four of the five main core strategies of any brokerage:

- Recruiting (very important)
- Retention & Loyalty
- Management
- Productivity

Peter Mueller

The FINANCIAL & OPERATIONS MANAGEMENT side involves the financial operations strategy of the brokerage, and includes:

- Compensation Model
- Budgeting
- Cash Flow
- Business Planning
- Improving Processes
- Reviewing Numbers (Key Performance Indicators (KPIs) score carding)

We may think that recruiting is the most important strategy to implement, however if we hire the wrong agents with low productivity who are on the wrong compensation program, we will recruit ourselves into bankruptcy. Notice that the recruiting is on the SALES side of the coin. The compensation model is on the financial operations side of the coin.

Both sides of the coin need to be addressed, not one at the expense of the other. You can also look at this using the analogy of a car. A car needs to have a gas pedal and brakes. The gas pedal is the SALES side of the coin. The brakes are the FINANCIAL OPERATIONS side of the coin. You need both to drive effectively.

What you measure gets improved!

When you think of the phrase Key Performance Indicators, or KPIs for short, think in terms of what drives the performance for your brokerage. There are several indicators that we ought to measure that drive performance:

- agent count
- agent attrition
- net agent growth
- gross profit
- expenses
- net profit

From my experience, more than ninety percent of the brokers I have spoken to and have worked with did not have a clear understanding of gross profit and did not know how to find it. The fact is that most income statements are not set up properly to indicate what I feel is the most important number in our business— gross profit.

If nothing else, recognize that the SALES side of the coin makes you money and the FINANCIAL OPERATIONS side of the coin makes you PROFIT.

THE PROFITABILITY BUSINESS MODEL™

The Profitability Business Model™ is a model we developed at The Profit Centre. It is the model we use to guide our brokers to build strong and profitable businesses. We developed this model over a number of years. By studying the most successful brokers in the industry, we started to see a consistent pattern and then defined what it was that set them apart.

Unfortunately, the more successful brokers are not always the obvious ones. Again, the reason for that is that we typically only acknowledge and celebrate volume. I know countless smaller brokerages that out-perform larger brokerages significantly in profitability.

The Profitability Business Model™ is made up of 9 Levels which represent the building blocks that lead you to the pinnacle of the model: Greater Profitability.

I'd like to explain and guide you through the 9 Levels of this model by using an illustration and an example from my own brokerage experience. Let me show you how I tripled my net profits in twelve months—even though I lost ten agents—and did not raise my fees.

I discovered that the basis for that success was founded on the understanding that sales and business are two distinct and different things. I also realized that if I did not invest in myself and my education, I would never have experienced the results that I am describing.

The transformation of my brokerage started with Level 1: The Profitability Mindset

LEVEL 1:
THE PROFITABILITY MINDSET

(1) / PROFITABILITY MINDSET \

The Profitability Mindset is the foundation of the Profitability Business Model™. The foundation is the most important aspect of any model or building. If the foundation is not wide and strong, anything you build on top of it will eventually fall to the ground. That means all the effort that is put into the rest of the building is weak and subject to collapse. When something collapses, it needs to be built up again which requires a tremendous amount of effort and time.

I have studied time and again that the most profitable brokers had this mindset. They did not capitulate to their agents. They had clarity and understanding. At the end of the day, the tail did not wag the dog, as the saying goes. They stood fast to their business model.

They created offices with a unique and powerful culture. When a leader is strong, it is felt. It makes the environment excellent to work in.

> *"When a leader is weak, the environment is weak, and the culture is poor."*
> —Peter Mueller

When I first started my brokerage in 1994. I did not have the Profitability Business Model™ to follow. I built my business on a weak foundation. That foundation was price. It needed to be more focused on value and on profit. I had no idea how to budget for profit. I had no idea what it could look like when it was done.

The profitability mindset is focused on learning, networking, and growth. For me, it was about an evolution in how I went from thinking like a salesperson to thinking like a businessperson. This led me to make that paradigm shift in my mind that was necessary for me to grow and learn how to be profitable. I always knew that I needed to invest in myself and that's when I enrolled in business coaching and training. This experience opened my eyes to the fact that I needed to recruit quality agents that contributed to my bottom line, as opposed to recruiting just for the sake of recruiting.

You must decide what's important to you and what you want to create. When you build a brokerage, your goal is to create equity and value as I mentioned in The

5 Purposes of a Business. Build your business as if you were going to sell it.

When I had sixty sales associates, I realized that I was not attaining the level of profitability that I desired. I paid myself a $120,000 salary as an employee of my own business, and I was making $50,000 in net profit. For the amount of work and risk I was putting in, I was not excited about the results. That's when I sought out the help of a business professional. It was the best decision I ever made.

My coach helped me look at my business like a business and not operate it with a salesperson mentality. He put me on the right path to be successful in my brokerage business.

The most profound thing he taught me was that I wasn't measuring all the right numbers. He taught me that one of the most important numbers that I should be measuring was my *gross profit per agent.*

That was the most important number to define and measure. I took that to heart. All he did was seed that one thought. That seed germinated and grew in my head, and everything evolved from there. That led me to Level 2: Clarity.

LEVEL 2: CLARITY

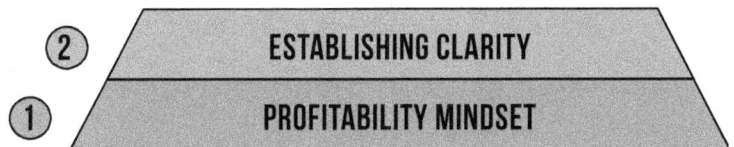

Clarity was what I discovered was missing in the running my business. It had to do with understanding my business numbers. There are many numbers in the brokerage business which we can study and measure. Once again, the main issue was that I was not measuring the *return* on volume numbers. Instead, I was measuring volume numbers such as sales volume, gross commission income, transactions, and agent count. I certainly was not measuring profit, not to mention gross profit!

What is Gross Profit? Well, it is the amount of money that's left over after you pay your agents their portion of the gross commissions per transaction, plus any royalty fees. It is also the money you make from ancillary revenue.

The first thing I had to determine was how much gross profit was I making annually.

When I looked at my financials, I found that I had approximately $420,000 in gross profit. At the time, I had approximately sixty sales associates working in my brokerage. When I divided the sixty sales associates into the $420,000 gross profit number, the result was that I was earning $7,000 in gross profit per agent on average for that year.

Gross Profit:	*$420,000*
No. of Agents	*<u>/60 agents</u>*
Gross Profit Per Agent:	*$ 7,000*

I learned this piece of valuable information from my coach. I found it interesting how that one seed of thought naturally guided me to my next thought, and I asked myself, what does my Gross Profit Per Agent (GPPA) need to look like for me to get excited about my business? I thought, okay, if I could get my average to $10,000 GPPA and then multiply that by the sixty agents, that would get me $600,000 in gross profit.

At the time I had $370,000 in expenses, which included paying myself $120,000 for salary as an employee of my company. After factoring in these numbers, I concluded that I would earn $230,000 in net profit.

Gross Profit:	*$600,000*
Operational Costs	*-$370,000*
Net Profit	*=$230,000*

Now that got me excited! That got me up in the morning. Step one was to determine what I wanted. What would make it worth my while?

To figure this out, I had to ask myself "If I need to earn $10,000 in GPPA per year, on average, how many of my existing agents are already earning me that?"

To come up with the answer, I put a list together of the sixty agents I had at the time and noted beside each name how much I was earning from each one of them.

When I did that, I realized that thirty-three of the sixty agents were earning me more than $10,000 in gross profit, and twenty-seven of my agents were earning me less than $10,000 in gross profit. In summary, 55% of my agents were above my goal and 45% of the agents were below my goal.

33 agents (55%) above $10,000
in GPPA average
27 agents (45%) below $10,000
in GPPA average

Next step was to total up the revenue for the top 55%.

33 agents = $360,000 or 86% of the total
$420,000 in Gross Profit

The results for the bottom 45% of my agents were:

27 agents = $60,000 or 14% of the total
$420,000 in Gross Profit

Wow! 86% of my gross profit came from the top 55% of my office and only 14% of my gross profit came from the bottom 45% of my agents.

Once I had that clarity and saw the results, I immediately realized that even if I lost the twenty-seven agents on the bottom, the worst thing that would happen is that I would only lose 14% of my gross profit. Wow!

So, if the worst-case scenario is that I lose the twenty-seven agents at the bottom, why do I feel the need to kowtow to them?

Even worse, if I need to earn more money, why would I raise the fees for everybody to achieve my goal as opposed to just raising the fees for the bottom 14%? The worst thing that can happen is that they leave, and that's ok.

It's amazing what happens when you have clarity. When you know the right numbers to measure, and when you do a little analysis.

To reiterate, all this insight began with just that one new seed of thought from my coach. You need to measure the right numbers, one of them being your GPPA.

SUMMARY:

LEVEL 1: THE PROFITABILITY MINDSET

With proper education, we can change our mindset to think more like a businessperson and focus our attention to building profit—not just making sales.

LEVEL 2: ESTABLISHING CLARITY

When you have clarity in your numbers, the insights that it gives you are profound. You can therefore quickly recognize the problem. Only when you identify the real problem can you come up with a real solution.

LEVEL 3: BUDGETING FOR PROFIT

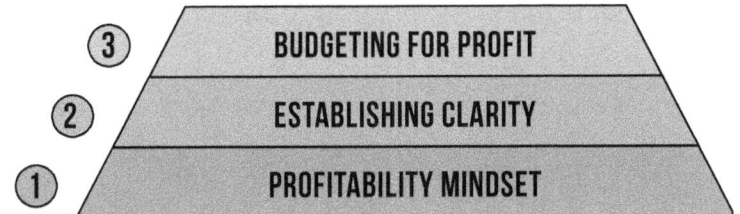

L et's take a deeper dive into Level 3: Budgeting for Profit.

If you recall, I determined that I would like to earn: $10,000 in GPPA per year.

If I could earn that with 60 agents, I would have: $600,000 in gross profit.

60 agents x $10,000 Gross Profit per Agent = $600,000 in total Gross Profit

With $370,000 in expenses, that would leave me with

$230,000 in net profit.

$600,000 Gross Profit - $370,000 Operational
Expenses = $230,000 Net Profit

In addition to that, I realized that if I can achieve that goal, I would have a business that could be worth $1,000,000. Now that's what I call equity.

It's very motivating when one realizes that earning a net profit, also creates equity! As I shared in The 5 Purposes of a Business, purpose number five is to have something to eventually sell.

So, notice the chronological order of the process again.

Level 1: The Profitability Mindset

You first must have a profitability mindset and a hunger to learn to become a businessperson, not just a salesperson.

Level 2: Establishing Clarity

Then you must then have clarity of your numbers. Numbers that give you real insight and ultimately inspire you.

Level 3: Budgeting for Profit

Notice how the clarity of your numbers automatically takes you to the next step which is Budgeting for Profit.

Peter Mueller

LEVEL 4: FINANCIAL MISSION & VISION

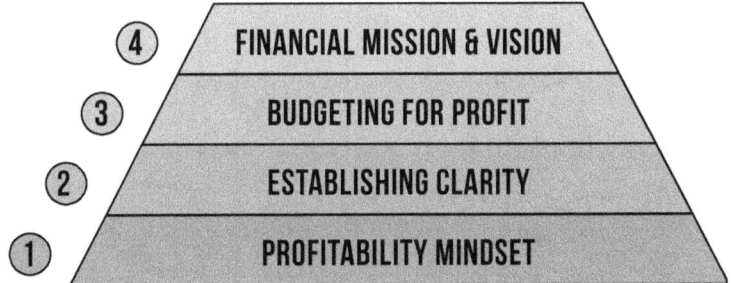

U sually, when we speak about a mission and a vision, we are referring to a declaration of a company's purpose and core values. It describes what a company does and who receives its valuable products or services. An effective mission statement motivates team members to work towards a shared goal.

When I refer to Financial Mission & Vision, I am referring to the ultimate value and outcome of the operations.

With this newfound perspective I identified my Financial Mission & Vision the following way:

My Financial Mission was to grow to:

60 sales associates that average:
$10,000 in GPPA per year

that will generate:

$600,000 in total gross profit

to maintain:

$370,000 in operation expenses

which will result in:

$230,000 net profit

which will create:

Approximately $1,000,000 in Equity

Now that's what I call a Financial Mission.

My Financial Vision refers to something that I would like to ultimately achieve within the next five years.

My Financial Vision was to grow to:

100 sales associates that average:
$10,000 in GPPA per year

that will generate:

$1,000,000 in total gross profit

to maintain:

$425,000 in operation expenses

which will achieve:

$575,000 Net Profit

which will create:

Approximately $1,750,000 in Equity

Now that's Level 4! We can see how this progression works. Once again, we haven't even talked about how to do it yet and that's okay.

I'm going to show you how I did it with my brokerage, but notice that I didn't start with the strategy, I didn't just start with the recruiting. If you start with the strategy which is Level 7 ultimately, you're not going to have the right objective. You need to establish the right mindset.

Without this clearly defined declaration, you will not attract the right agent. You will not achieve whatever goal you think you may have. Most brokers never had that vision or that perspective.

When we create a financial mission and vision document, it will provide true motivation because the outcomes are realistic and clearly defined. When my goal was simply to recruit more agents, and I only defined how many I wanted, then when I achieved that objective, I was very dissatisfied.

Ultimately, your goals have to be on the right thing, otherwise they will not motivate the right behaviours. When I clearly defined them as I described, I was laser focused on recruiting my "ideal agent," as opposed to any agent.

Now that I had a clearly defined Financial Mission & Vision, the next step was obvious. I needed to align my financial model (my compensation programs) to achieve the result.

LEVEL 5:
ALIGNMENT

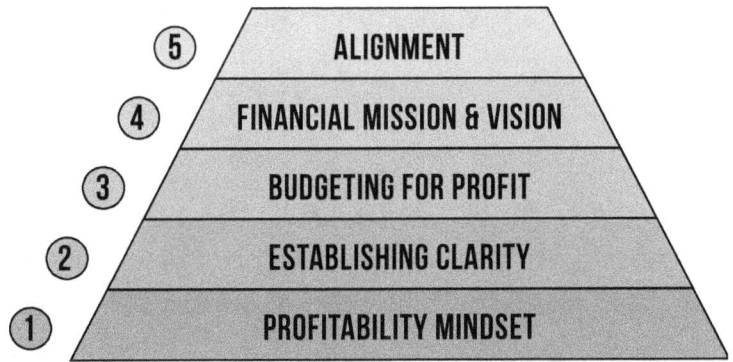

Now that a Financial Mission & Vision has been set, we can move on to alignment.

Knowing that I wanted to earn $10,000 in GPPA per year to achieve my financial mission, I had to figure out how to align my compensation plans to achieve my goal.

I realized that for 55% of my agents (thirty-three of them), there was no problem at all. They were able to achieve the $10,000 GPPA objective every single year and then some.

I realized due to clarity, that it was the twenty-seven agents who were below my objective that were not in alignment. So, what did that mean?

I needed to change the way I was charging them!

The top 55% of my agents were pulling their weight. They didn't deserve to pay more. It was with the bottom 45% of my agents that I needed to make some changes to their compensation plans.

It's a danger if you arbitrarily raise fees. The ones you hurt the most are your top-producing agents. That is not the right approach to increasing revenues. This is also a classic reason why low-producing agents cost you a fortune.

By not addressing the true underlying issue of low production, we will tend to make bad decisions and allow these agents to wallow year after year. I have heard brokers over the years say things like, "Well, they don't bother me. At least I make a few thousand dollars from them every year." Wrong! You will lose hundreds of thousands of dollars having that attitude and management style! It will cost you a fortune.

I have witnessed time and again the huge cost of inadequate management. When I advise my clients to have more one-on-one accountability meetings with their agents the response I would often get is, "I don't have the time." May I suggest that the reason why they did not have time was because they were not profitable?

If they are not profitable, they are unable to afford the salaries necessary to run a successful brokerage.

Once again, Purpose 2 from The 5 Purposes of a Business is Leverage.

My compensation program at the time was to charge $250 a month or $3,000 a year and charge a $1,000 transaction fee for the first seven transactions in the contract year. After seven transactions, the transaction fee would be only $395 for the balance of the contract year.

In summary, if an agent does seven transactions, they will achieve my GPPA objective of $10,000 per agent per year minimum.

$7,000 in transaction fees + $3,000 in fixed monthly fees.

The compensation program I had in place was adequate. The problem of course, was that not every agent was doing seven transactions per year. I needed to come up with a strategy for getting the bottom 45% of my agents to pay at least $7,000 in transaction fees.

That meant that I needed to adjust the fee structure (for just that group) so that I would obtain the $7,000 quicker and on fewer transactions.

I quickly realized that all I had to do was take a higher transaction fee upfront for the bottom 45%, depending on where they were in the contract year. It wasn't a very difficult sell because most of those agents believed they could achieve that minimum production standard of seven transactions. They knew that regardless of when those transactions closed that they would not be paying any more than anyone else. The risk to the brokerage was mitigated by taking the fees sooner.

As simplistic as this may sound, I would have never come up with such a strategy unless I had the previous four levels identified.

Level 1: The Profitability Mindset
Level 2: Establishing Clarity
Level 3: Budgeting for Profit
Level 4: Financial Mission and Vision
To reach:
Level 5: Alignment
Alignment of the compensation structure.

LEVEL 6:
VALUE PROPOSITION

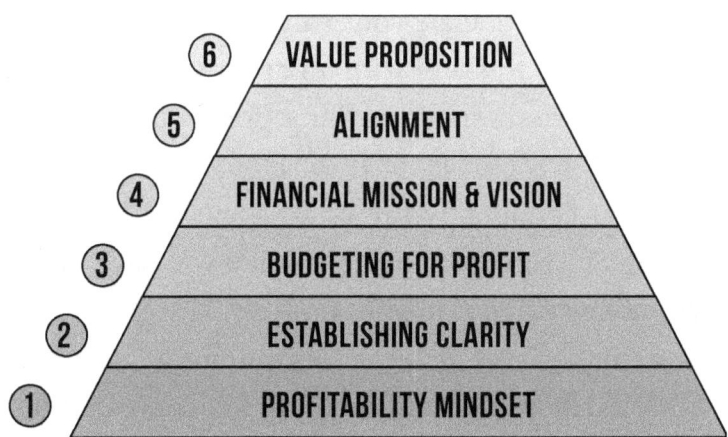

Your Value Proposition should clearly define your values and especially your points of distinction from your competitors. Your Value Proposition is what's needed to support your compensation programs. Therefore, Value Proposition shows up at Level 6.

I found that only after identifying all these points of distinction with a broker, we found that we were underselling ourselves. It is important to take time to not only identify your Value Proposition, but also to enhance it.

If you cannot define what makes you different, then why would someone choose to work in your office? In the absence of value, price is the only issue.

You need to identify and create a value proposition so powerful that it will overcome any objections agents might have to not join your office. Can you confidently and effectively articulate your value?

Are you able to share with an agent why they would generate more money working for you than anywhere else?

Can you confidently say to an agent, "What's more important to you, how much money you save or how much money you put in your pocket?"

I strengthen my value proposition by looking at what would help agents make more sales and ultimately more profit.

By using my value proposition, I wanted to be able to say to an agent I was trying to recruit, "If I could show you that you would make an additional $50,000 or $100,000 a year working at my office compared to where you are now, would you join us?"

I have found that many brokers do a horrible job of presenting their value proposition. Overloading an agent with everything that you and your office does is not a good way to sell it.

The most important thing to consider is that every agent can be different. We all have our lives, our stories, and our values. When I mentioned earlier in this book that I was motivated by acknowledgement, it is important to realize that not everybody is motivated that way. The bottom line is that the only way to understand what makes someone tick is to be prepared to ask many questions.

The second thing to do is to listen.

Only by asking questions and listening will we be able to identify what would be most important to that individual.

For example, let's say that we discovered that an agent, let's call him Sam, complained that they did not receive good training, or was never guided in building an effective business plan.

Let us assume that you have great training and know how to build a business plan for agents. The danger at this stage is to just blurt it out and say that we offer that.

At this point, I would like to share with you a process I created called Quantifying Your Points of Distinction.

Using the above example, the first question I would ask is, "Sam, what would you say is your average gross commission income on a transaction?"

Let's say he said, "$10,000."

I would then say the following, "Sam, in our conversation you mentioned that training was important to you. You also mentioned that you felt a business plan would help you in your career, is that correct?"

At this stage, I would show Sam our training curriculum and an example of a comprehensive business plan.

I would say, "Sam, as you can see, we provide excellent training, and I can help you build a comprehensive business plan. Would you agree with me that if we could help you with those two things and keep you accountable to your plan, you would generate more sales?"

If the answer is yes, I would then ask, "How many additional sales would you say you would generate if you were assisted in these items?"

Please take note! I did not tell Sam that he would make more money, I asked him how many additional sales he thought he would generate if he were provided those services.

Let's say he said five additional sales.

The average gross commission income per transaction in our area at the time was $10,000. Therefore, I multiplied that by five to get $50,000.

Can you imagine doing this process with four or five items from your value proposition? Based on the above, my final statement would be somewhat tongue in cheek. "Sam, I have good news and bad news. The good news is that based solely on our projected calculations, you would earn an additional $50,000. The bad news is that we charge a little more than your current brokerage by about $3,000, so you only get to keep an additional $47,000. Is that okay with you?"

I hope that gives you a good start for identifying your value and additionally how to quantify your points of distinction.

What's next?

LEVEL 7:
STRATEGY

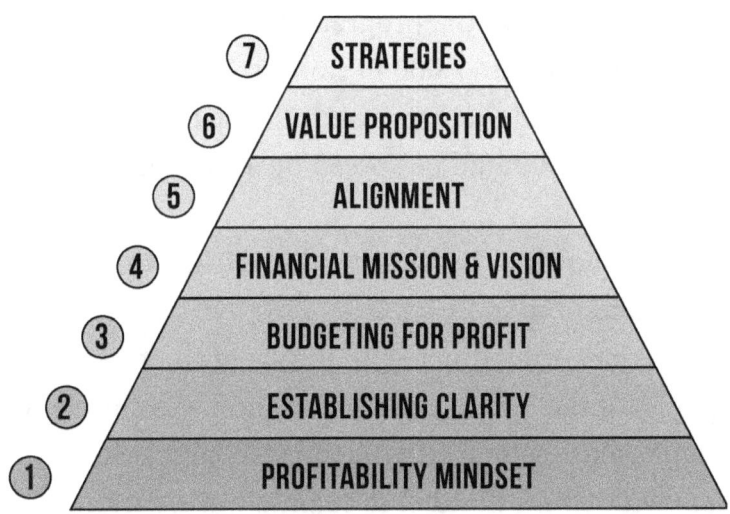

W hat was the strategy that I implemented?

My goal was to increase my average GPPA from $7,000 per year to $10,000 per year. It was a very simple and clear-cut goal.

To review; 55% of my agents did not need any adjustment, however, 45% of my agents did.

Here is the action plan I came up with:

Step 1: Sit down with every agent in my office two months before their contract anniversary date to review their performance.

Because the contract anniversary dates were based on when they joined the office, it was easy to spread out the conversations accordingly.

Step 2: Have the bottom 45% of the agents sign off on any revisions to the program guaranteeing that they pay a minimum of $7,000 in transaction fees within the twelve months of their renewed contract.

The strategy would be spread over the twelve months to fully execute.

The following is what the sit-down meeting looked like.

It was easy to sit down with the agents that were in the top 55% of the office. The conversation was simply this: "Thanks for meeting with me today. I have good news to share with you. I decided to maintain the current compensation program for you and not increase fees. The reason I can do this is that you are exceeding my GPPA objective. I want you to know however that the agents that are not pulling their weight will be paying the difference. Thank you for being part of our team."

By the way, those agents were quite impressed with the approach and fully supported the strategy. It made them feel important and it made them feel that we were committed to creating a culture of winners. They were impressed knowing that I was not going to allow low productivity and weakness to infiltrate our culture and our environment or allow it to create some sort of socialistic entity.

For the agents that were in the bottom 45% of my office, the conversation was a little different. It sounded something like this: "Thank you for meeting with me today. Contract renewal is coming up and I wanted to share with you some good news and some bad news. The good news is that I am not changing the compensation program fees. The bad news is that I will be keeping you accountable for paying a minimum of $7,000 in annual transaction fees whether you do seven transactions or not. I am going to give you a pass for the previous twelve months, however moving forward if you choose to stay with me, you will be responsible for hitting that target. Now, you can do seven transactions, don't you agree?"

If they answered no, I suggested that it would be best that we part ways. If they answered yes, I would tell them that I would help them achieve that minimum goal by helping them to build a business plan and to guide them through it with accountability and training. I then had them commit to that in writing by having them sign an amendment to the previous agreement.

Here is an example of what happened to an agent I had in that bottom 45%:

That agent just closed their first transaction in six months. The transaction fee we took was not $1,000, it was $3,500 because that was the minimum amount that we should have collected in six months.

Essentially what I was doing was putting the monkey on the back of the agent, where it belonged.

Step 3: After we started implementing the strategy, we started to measure monthly the production and the GPPA. Every month I knew who was falling behind. We measured the agents' goals versus the actuals. I knew every month who was in the black and who was in the red. If an agent fell in the red by a certain amount, I would schedule an accountability meeting with them. I was still committed to their success. I didn't want them to fall too far behind and on some occasions, I decided that it was best that they left.

Step 4: Whenever there was a closing, my office administrator would calculate the transaction fee according to the status of the agent involved in line with their amended agreement.

These were the four steps that were implemented to accomplish the results that I wanted to achieve for my office.

How did I measure those results? Well, that takes us to the next level, Level 8, which is Measure.

LEVEL 8: MEASURE

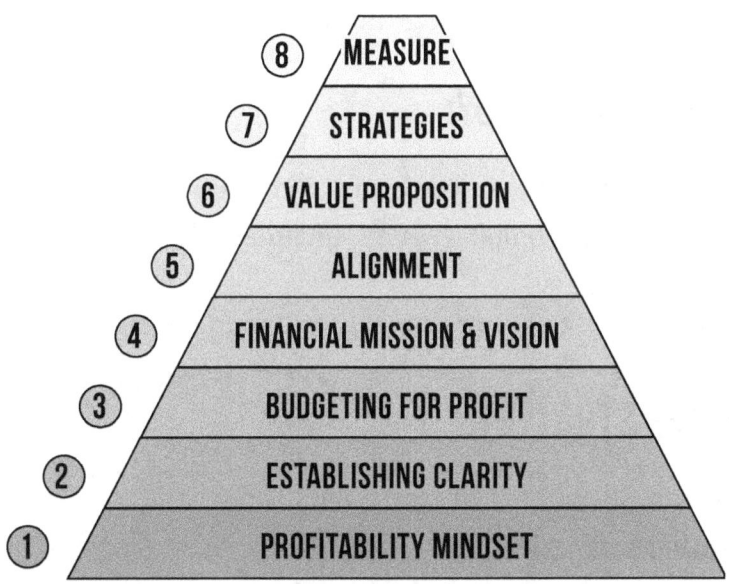

⑧	MEASURE
⑦	STRATEGIES
⑥	VALUE PROPOSITION
⑤	ALIGNMENT
④	FINANCIAL MISSION & VISION
③	BUDGETING FOR PROFIT
②	ESTABLISHING CLARITY
①	PROFITABILITY MINDSET

What you measure gets improved! These famous words were coined by many famous individuals, one of whom was management strategist Peter Drucker. This is such a powerful and fundamental truth.

For your brokerage, one of the things that you will want to measure are your Key Performance Indicators (KPIs).

A KPI is every and any number that drives performance. Concerning this strategy, the key driver identified is Gross Profit Per Agent (GPPA).

After implementing my four step strategy in Level 7, I did end up with some fallout, meaning I did lose a few agents from the bottom 45%.

Let me show you how everything looked after twelve months of implementing the strategy:

BEFORE STRATEGY:

Agents: 60 agents Gross Profit: $420,000
Expenses: $370,000 (which included the $120,000 in manager salary)
Net Profit = $420,000 – $370,000 = $50,000

AFTER STRATEGY:

Agents: 50 agents (10 agents left)
Gross Profit: $516,000
Expenses: $350,000 (which included the $120,000 in manager salary)
Net Profit: $516,000 – $350,000 = $166,000

I more than tripled my net profits with ten fewer agents—and I didn't increase fees.

But wait, there's more. Don't forget that creating a business that generates true net profit also creates equity as we mentioned in Level 4.

The net profit increase grew from $50,000 to $166,000.

That is an increase of $110,000 or *332%*.

It would be a fair estimate that an additional $110,000 in net profit improved the equity position of the company by at least $350,000.

Net profit plus equity equals value. Therefore, after the implementation of the above-mentioned strategy, we created an additional $350,000 in equity plus $166,000 in net profit for a total value of $516,000 in only twelve months. If that doesn't encourage change, I don't know what else will.

LEVEL 9:
IMPROVE

9 IMPROVE

8 MEASURE

7 STRATEGIES

6 VALUE PROPOSITION

5 ALIGNMENT

4 FINANCIAL MISSION & VISION

3 BUDGETING FOR PROFIT

2 ESTABLISHING CLARITY

1 PROFITABILITY MINDSET

Level 9 is at the pinnacle of our Profitability Business Model™. It represents the outcome of implementing Levels 1 through 8 successfully.

I would never have tripled my net profits had I simply stayed the way I was. All of this came about by executing The 9 Levels to Greater Profitability and measuring an elusive number called Gross Profit Per Agent.

Level 9 is the accomplishment and reward of a successful strategy. Once we attain this level, we can enjoy the results, but we will never just stay there.

Running an effective business means revisiting Level 7, which is building additional strategies, measuring them, and then improving other areas of our brokerage.

It's a constant cycle of going through Level 7 to Level 9. Strategies, measure, improve, strategies, measure, improve . . .

That is how you build a brokerage on a solid foundation.

SUMMARY

I would like you to keep in mind that even though the scenario I shared with you is from my personal experiences, the lessons I learned from it can be applied universally. The fundamentals are applicable to any brokerage.

Your numbers may be different than mine were, and even mine have changed over time due to inflation, but the fundamentals do not change.

There is no question that greater profitability was the result of executing the Levels as set forth in the Profitability Business Model™.

There are five core areas in your brokerage that need to be addressed to produce sustainable and repeatable results:

1. Management
2. Financial
3. Productivity
4. Retention & Loyalty
5. Recruiting

In my example strategy, I touched on the management, financial, and production elements of the business. I didn't discuss much about retention and recruiting. The reason I mention this is because, from my experience in consulting and coaching, the areas that we did address are the areas that are the most neglected ones.

Therefore, the common issue is Profitability. To address it, we must be open to both sides of the coin in managing profitability as we mentioned earlier in this book.

Let's do a quick recap of The 9 Levels according to the example given.

LEVEL 1: THE PROFITABILITY MINDSET

Having a profitability mindset is the foundation of your success. I would never have come this far without it. It is having a desire for growth and not being satisfied with the status quo. The constant pursuit of growth and learning is what helped create this profitability mindset.

I have worked with enough brokers to know how stuck they can get when they rely solely on what is in their heads and execute only very basic strategies. The constant pursuit of knowledge and expertise was the foundation to the insights and the results I managed to attain.

I can't imagine how I would have evolved if it wasn't for my coach and business mentor.

LEVEL 2: CLARITY

Understanding GPPA was what gave me the awareness of the true issue with my profitability. Being given the right seed of an idea by my coach was all it took for me to get it to germinate and grow. It is incredible how having the right kind of information can set you on the right path.

At the end of the day, I truly didn't know what I didn't know. When I discovered that 86% of my gross profit was attained by only 55% of my agents, the ideas and thoughts started to flow. It didn't take long to start implementing some positive changes.

LEVEL 3: BUDGETING FOR PROFIT

I never budgeted for a profit before. I have only ever budgeted for expenses. Having a clear vision of what my profitability could be was the motivation I needed to turn things around and to stay engaged and excited about the opportunity of increasing my profits. In this case, it was by simply defining a basic objective, which was to increase my GPPA per year from $7,000 to $10,000.

LEVEL 4: FINANCIAL MISSION AND VISION

This understanding only put fuel on the fire. Identifying that I was not only building a profitable business, but I was also creating equity in my business really inspired and energized me!

What was frustrating for me was that I gave up a lucrative sales business to begin my brokerage, and I was not getting the results I wanted in exchange for my time and effort. Then, by focusing on equity and value I found the inner drive that helped me achieve my goals. *I knew that if I achieved my financial mission, I would be creating over $500,000 in value.*

LEVEL 5: ALIGNMENT

When the possibilities are laid out for you, as they were for me, then you will be able to identify what you need to do to adjust your compensation plans. I gained the confidence to make a bold move after I discovered what the worst case scenario would be and noticed that is was very minimal. That helped me improve my value proposition and strengthen my resolve as to what I wanted the business to look like and to not compromise my values for the sake of volume.

Staying true to the objective and having clarity about that objective, will give you the confidence to make bold changes and to persevere. Without that clear objective and how to achieve it, we would be very vulnerable and weak in validating our decisions. When we are weak in our decisions and objectives we will most likely capitulate to others.

Peter Mueller

LEVEL 6: VALUE PROPOSITION

This process forced me to enhance my value offering. I needed to justify my compensation programs and compete with my competitors. I needed to validate our changes so that we could sell our value with confidence, without having to capitulate to low-producing agents and let the tail wag the dog, so to speak. The stronger the value proposition, the stronger the presentation got.

The more I focused on value versus price, the easier it was for me to maintain the integrity of my values. and to be fully transparent. There were no hidden agendas, and everyone was treated fairly.

LEVEL 7: STRATEGY

The strategy was a simple one. It involved following through on only four steps.

1. Book an appointment with every agent two months before the contract date.
2. Have a prepared script for both categories of agents, one for those that were above the goal and one for those that were below the goal.
3. Measure GPPA monthly.
4. Administrate transaction fees accordingly.

LEVEL 8: MEASURE

In this example, the number we measured was GPPA.

LEVEL 9: IMPROVE

The proof is in the pudding. The results were outstanding. Yes, it was a calculated risk. But the risk was mitigated because it was based on the right information. To be quite honest, it didn't scare me a bit to implement my new strategy because I truly believed and knew that the agents that would appreciate it the most were the ones that generated 86% of the gross profit.

CONCLUSION

I would like to conclude this book by sharing and discussing one of my favourite quotes with you. It comes from one the most famous coaches of all time, Jim Rohn.

"When someone is going down the wrong road, they do not need the motivation to speed them up, they need the education to turn them around."

In my real estate career, I have attended and participated with many companies that promote training and coaching. I also attended many conferences and events. It didn't occur to me at the time that most of that training and self-improvement was only essentially focused on creating more volume.

I recall a broker who asked me to help him recruit more agents. I told him that I would be delighted to help. He had over two hundred agents at the time and on the surface, it certainly looked like he was very successful. I told him that before we begin recruiting, I wanted to look at his financials, his compensation plans, and his production.

His production (volume) was amazing, however his profit (return on volume) was nonexistent. Even worse, he was losing money.

After going through that analysis, I told him that if I helped him recruit more agents, things being as they were, I would be helping him to bankruptcy earlier.

That's why that quote has significance for me. When you start to walk in the light, you want to share that light with others.

That was the inspiration that founded The Profit Centre.

Solutions are never quick and easy, but the payoff will be great. What an opportunity it is to create a solid business model and then duplicate that model time and time again. What an opportunity it is to create an empire by simply using a proven model.

Brokerages are failing and struggling because the leadership is weak and the owners do not have a Profitability Mindset. What an opportunity to rescue that ship and embody strong leadership and values.

Profitability is simply the by-product of great leadership. People want to work for great leaders. I believe they hunger for it. What about YOU?

This is Peter Mueller signing off, wishing you all
A Profitable Day!

ABOUT THE AUTHOR

In 1984, at 19 years old, Peter began his career in real estate. Over the course of his career, he has been consistently recognized within the top 2% of sales and has also been recognized for his outstanding leadership.

At the age of 29, Peter founded his real estate firm and, in less than 3 years, grew his organization from a start-up to a profitable company with 60 sales professionals and staff. He led the implementation of all business processes, financial reporting, and controls to create a business with sustainable and repeatable cash flow. His talent for recruiting and generating new business was unmatched in the industry.

After selling his real estate company, Peter committed his career to guiding and consulting agents, teams, and brokers toward sustainable profitability.

He founded The Profit Centre in 2008. The mission statement of The Profit Centre is to passionately enhance people's lives by guiding them to greater profitability.

The Profit Centre through its experience working with over 1,000 brokerages around the world created a consulting process called the Profitability Business Model™. Part of this process included developing the "Profit Analysis". With over 1,000 profit analyses completed as of 2022, we stand alone as the authority on brokerage and team metrics, benchmarks, averages, and best practices.

As the founder and CEO of The Profit Centre, Peter speaks to thousands of brokers and agents annually. His clients span ten time zones and a host of countries and range from startups to large regional enterprises. He is passionate about helping agents, teams, brokers, and executives reach their profitability goals.

Peter Mueller